Motivating Thoughts Of Elon Musk

Motivating Thoughts Of Elon Musk

Edited by
RIDHIMA SHARMA

PRABHAT
PRAKASHAN

Published by
PRABHAT PRAKASHAN PVT. LTD.
4/19 Asaf Ali Road,
New Delhi-110002 (INDIA)
e-mail: prabhatbooks@gmail.com

ISBN 978-93-5521-772-1
MOTIVATING THOUGHTS OF ELON MUSK
Edited by Ridhima Sharma

Edition
First, 2023

Price
₹ 250 (Rupees Two Hundred Fifty Only)

Printed at
Japan Art, Delhi

Editor's Note

South African-born American business magnate, engineer and investor, Elon Reeve Musk doesn't need a special introduction as he is globally known for his ambitious goals and analytical thinking that has enabled him to achieve his near-to-impossible goals. From creating electric cars to launching a reusable rocket in space to introducing Hyperloop (a high-speed transportation system), there's not much that he can't achieve when he sets his mind to it.

On June 28, 1971, Elon Musk was born to a Canadian mother, Maye Musk and a South African father, Errol Musk in Pretoria, South Africa. He is the firstborn of his parents. He has a younger brother named Kimbal and a younger sister named Tosca. Musk belongs to a wealthy family where his mother is a renowned model and dietician, and his father is an electromechanical engineer, pilot, sailor, consultant, and property developer.

Musk is the owner and CEO of Twitter, Inc.; the founder of The Boring Company; the co-founder of Neuralink and

OpenAI; the CEO and chief engineer of SpaceX; an angel investor, the CEO and chief product architect of Tesla, Inc.; and the president of the charitable Musk Foundation. He was also the co-founder of the electronic payment firm, PayPal. In 2016, Tesla acquired SolarCity and transform its solar business into Tesla Energy.

From a young age, Musk was a fast learner and was interested in computer programming and engineering. Also, he has displayed an enterprising spirit from the beginning. Therefore, it is no surprise that he read the entire Encyclopedia Britannica by the age of nine, learned computer programming in three days, completed a double major in business and physics, built a video game called 'Blaster' at the age of twelve and so much more.

Having divorced parents and a different perspective from the other students of his age were the reasons why he often got bullied by his classmates. At the age of 17, Musk decided to move to Canada for further studies at Queen's University and also to avoid mandatory military service in South Africa. Later in 1992, he moved to the United States to study business and physics at the University of Pennsylvania. He holds a PhD degree in energy physics from Stanford University in California.

Musk is a visionary who believes in finding solutions to problems instead of lamenting about them. As he is deeply immersed in every aspect of his business, he is first and foremost an engineer by passion and an entrepreneur out of necessity. With his work, he has managed to accelerate the development of multi-planetary civilization and renewable energy.

Despite all trials and tribulations, Musk has exceeded people's expectations on various occasions. His ability to navigate problems of varied complexity has helped him to rise above mediocrity and achieve greater success in every field of his business. In this book, you will find the most inspiring quotes from Elon Musk which you may find enlightening and informative.

❑

Contents

Elon Musk: A Brief Biography

Elon Musk also known as Elon Reeve Musk is one of the greatest and most prolific modern inventors and is responsible for monumental advancements in futuristic technology like renewable energy and space travel. Many of his innovations seem to be out of a science-fiction movie, but throughout his career, he has brought huge scientific breakthroughs. After making his first fortune from the internet payment service 'PayPal', he invested $100 million in his space travel company 'SpaceX' and began building satellites, launch vehicles and other spacecraft both for NASA and for his own company, creating new milestones with his privately funded spacecraft.

Many of his revolutionary ideas and inventions focus on space travel, renewable energy, commercial electric cars and other technologies, that envisage a future where fossil fuels and other resources may be in shorter supply. His futuristic and visionary ideas have won him both scientific and philanthropic recognition and awards. Pop culture sometimes portrays him as a sort of real-life superhero, dedicated to providing worldwide solutions to international problems.

Musk looks to the future, hopes for intelligent life elsewhere in the universe and continues to plan far-reaching futuristic goals such as a human colony on Mars.

Childhood and Early Life

Elon Musk was born in Pretoria, South Africa on June 28, 1971. The oldest of three siblings with a prodigious family name, he grew up in the last decades of Apartheid.

His parents were Maye Musk, a British-Canadian model and Errol Musk, a South Africa-born British electrical engineer. When they divorced in 1980, Elon stayed mainly with his father in South Africa. A few years later, he began teaching himself computer programming and sold his first video game at the age of 12.

He attended Queen's University in Kingston, Ontario, for his undergraduate education, in 1990. He eventually transferred to the University of Pennsylvania, earning a dual degree in Physics and Economics.

In addition to the bachelor's degrees, he earned in physics and economics; he also holds an honorary doctorate in Design from the Art Centre College of Design and an honorary doctorate in Aerospace Engineering from the University of Surrey.

Career

He moved to California to attend Stanford for a PhD in applied physics in 1995 but quit within a few days to pursue his interests in avenues of technology and entrepreneurship. Later that year, he worked with his brother, Kimbal Musk, to develop the software company 'Zip2', which provided services to high-end newspaper clients like *The New York Times* and the *Chicago Tribune*.

After the successful sale of Zip2 to Compaq in 1999, Musk went straight into his next venture, an online financial service called X.com. Shortly after the company acquired a money transfer service called PayPal, through a merger, they began to focus their efforts exclusively on building this internet payment service. The success of PayPal led Musk to sell his stock in the company to eBay for $165 million.

In 2002, he invested millions in his third company Space Exploration Technologies or just 'SpaceX'. Within seven years, the company had designed the Falcon line of space launch vehicles and the Dragon line of multi-purpose spacecraft and was making history with their privately funded innovation. SpaceX received contracts from NASA to create a launch craft to deliver cargo to the International Space Station.

Tesla Motors was founded with the mission of designing and building electric cars. Musk invested in the company and became its chairman in 2004, a year after its inception, taking on an active role in the design of the Roadster, which won the Global Green product award. During the recession when the company was adversely affected, he went on to become the CEO and product architect of the company, a role he holds till today.

After designing the initial concept for SolarCity, Musk remains its biggest shareholder. Today, it is the second-largest provider of solar energy in the United States, with a focus on combating global warming.

On August 12, 2013, Musk announced revolutionary plans for a high-speed travel technology that, in theory, could replace aeroplane travel as a faster and cheaper option. His company SpaceX is currently working on putting his plans into practice, with the design intended to run entirely on solar energy.

He envisioned a high-speed transportation system known as the Hyperloop. It incorporates reduced-pressure tubes in which pressurized capsules ride on air bearings driven by linear induction motors and air compressors.

In July 2017, he announced that the first successful test run of Hyperloop had been done in Nevada, USA. He also said that he had got verbal approval to build a hyperloop from New York City to Washington D.C.

Major Works

SpaceX has completed several contracts for NASA, sending its Falcon 9 spacecraft to the International Space Station with cargo. This spacecraft replaced the space shuttle when it retired in 2011.

Musk was heavily involved in the design of Tesla Motors' first electric sports car, the Tesla Roadster. He received the 2006 Global Green product design award for this vehicle, presented by Mikhail Gorbachev.

Personal Life and Legacy

Elon Musk has married thrice and twice to the same woman. His first marriage was to Canadian author Justine Wilson in 2000. They had six children together: all sons. Their first son, Nevada Alexander Musk, died at the age of 10 weeks due to sudden infant death syndrome. The couple had five more sons through IVF; twins in 2004, followed by triplets in 2006. Later, the couple divorced in 2008.

In 2008, he began dating English actress, Talulah Riley, and the two of them got married in 2010. The couple separated in 2012.

In 2013, Elon Musk remarried Talulah Riley but the couple filed for divorce in 2014, and it was finalized in 2016.

Elon Musk was briefly in a relationship with American actress Amber Heard in 2016, but the couple split owing to their conflicting schedules.

In 2018, Musk and Canadian musician Grimes revealed that they were dating. The couple had two children together; a boy named X AE A-XII in 2020 and a girl named Exa Dark in December 2021. Despite the pregnancy, the couple announced their separation in September 2021.

In July 2022, the Insider reports that Musk had twins with Shivon Zilis, the director of operations and special projects of Neuralink, in November 2021. Given that Zilis reported directly to Musk, this piece of news raised many questions about the workplace ethics of Neuralink.

❑

Quotes of Elon Musk

Achievement

- The size of the company's market cap isn't a metric by which I would judge my achievement.
- That was awesome. We made it to orbit, thanks to the hard work of the SpaceX team and all you guys. There were many people who thought we couldn't do it but as the saying goes, "fourth time's the charm." This means a great deal to SpaceX as getting to orbit is a huge milestone. There are only a handful of countries on earth that have done this. It is normally a country thing, not a company thing. So, it is an amazing achievement.
- I do worry about ensuring that we can achieve affordability thresholds, because even if you make

the value for money infinite if people do not have enough money to buy it then they still can't.

Acronym

- The key test for an acronym is to ask whether it helps or hurts communication.

Action

- I think what matters, is the actions I take, not what people think of me in the future. I'll be long dead. But the actions that I take, will they have been useful?
- We are just looking for any possible action that can improve the probability of success, no matter how small. Whether that comes from an intern or me or anyone, doesn't matter.
- If someone is given a trusted place in society, such as a police officer or a judge, and they are corrupt then we must be extra vigilant against such situations and should take action against it.

Alone

- As a child, I hated being alone. As an adult, I don't want to be alone. It makes one miserable.
- I will never be happy without having someone. Going to sleep alone kills me.

- When I was a child, there's one thing I said: 'I never want to be alone.' That's what I would say. I don't want to be alone.

America

- The United States is a nation of explorers. The people came here from other parts of the world that chose to give up the known in favour of the unknown. I think the United States is a distillation of the spirit of human exploration.
- We need to make sure our immigration laws are not unkind or unreasonable.
- The United States is ahead in the culture of innovation. If someone wants to accomplish great things, there is no better place than the US.
- The US automotive industry has been selling cars the same way for over 100 years, and there are many laws in place to govern exactly how that is to be accomplished.
- The rumours of the demise of the US manufacturing industry are greatly exaggerated.
- In the United States especially, there is an over-allocation of talent in finance and law. I think we should have fewer people doing finance and law and more people making stuff.

- I think a lot of the American people feel more than a little disappointed that the high-water mark for human exploration was 1969. The dream of human space travel has almost died for many people.

Appreciate

- You want to take a moment to appreciate things in life and the sensations. Food is incredible and there are just so many good things you can experience. Some of them cost nothing—have a walk-in nature, just a pleasant meal, and it is like, wow, that's most enjoyable. We should take a moment to appreciate these little things, big things, and good things that move our hearts. I think that is probably the meaning of life, as close a definition as I could think.

Artificial Intelligence

- I think we should be very careful about artificial intelligence. If I had to guess what our biggest existential threat is, it's probably that. So, we need to be very careful. With artificial intelligence, we are summoning the demon and being exposed to it.
- I have exposure to the most cutting-edge AI, and I think people should be concerned about it.
- The danger of AI is going to be more humans using it against each other, I think.
- My view on AI is essential, you can view the advancement of AI as solving things with increasing

degrees of freedom. So, the thing with the most degrees of freedom is real. But AI is steadily advanced, solving things that have more and more degrees of freedom. So obviously, it is something like checkers.

- AI does not need to hate us to destroy us.
- AI could be terrible, and it could be great. It is not clear. But one thing is for sure; we will control it.
- With artificial intelligence, we are summoning the demon. You know all those stories where there's the man with the pentagram and the holy water, and he's sure he can control the demon. It doesn't work out.
- I do think there should be some regulations on AI.
- One of the biggest mistakes we made was trying to automate things that are super easy for a person to do but super hard for a robot to do.
- I think AI is going to be incredibly sophisticated in 20 years. It seems to be accelerating. The tricky thing about predicting things when there is an exponential is that an exponential looks linear close-up. But actually, it is not linear. And AI appears to be accelerating, as far as I can see.
- Digital super-intelligence, I think, has the potential to be more dangerous than a nuclear bomb, so somebody should be keeping an eye on it. We can't have the inmates running the asylum.

- Hope we are not just the biological boot loader for digital super-intelligence. Unfortunately, that is increasingly probable.
- AI is a fundamental existential risk for human civilization and I don't think people fully appreciate that.
- It feels like we are the biological bootloader for AI, effectively. We are building it. And then, we are building progressively greater intelligence, and the percentage of intelligence that is not human is increasing, and eventually, we will represent a very small percentage of intelligence.
- It is not as though I think that the risk is that the AI would develop entirely on its own right off the bat. The concern is that someone may use it in a pernicious, and even if they weren't going to use it in a destructive way, somebody could take it from them and use it in a negative way. That, I think, is quite a big danger. We must have democratization of AI technology and make it widely available. That is the reason we created OpenAI.
- There is a quote that I love from Lord Acton—he was the man who came up with, "Power corrupts and absolute power corrupts absolutely"—which is that "freedom consists of the distribution of power and despotism in its concentration." I think it is important

that we have this incredible power of AI that is not concentrated in the hands of the few.

Assets

- I have a number of houses, but I don't spend much time in most of them, and that doesn't seem like optimum use of assets; somebody could probably be enjoying those houses and getting better use of them than myself.
- I think possessions tend to weigh you down; they are a kind of attack vector.

Attention

- You can train yourself to pay attention to the minuscule details; I think almost anyone can. This is very much a double-edged sword because then you see all the minute details, and then trifling things drive you berserk.

Attitude

Generally, I look for a positive attitude; are they easy to work with or are people going to like working with them? It is very important to like the people you work with, otherwise, your life and job are going to be quite miserable. We have a strict no-jerks policy at SpaceX. We fire people if they are jerks. I mean, we do give them an initial warning but if they continue to be jerks then they are fired.

❑

Battery

- A battery by definition is a collection of cells. So, the cell is a small can of chemicals. And the challenge is taking a very high-energy cell, and several of them, and combining them safely into a large battery.
- I do think batteries are one of the hardest technology problems out there because there are so many constraints on creating a useful battery. So many super smart people have broken their pick on improving batteries. It usually ends up being, on average, about a 5 to 8 per cent improvement per year in energy density and economics.
- My top advice for anyone who says they have got some breakthrough battery technology is please send us (Tesla) a sample cell. Don't send us a PowerPoint. Just send us one cell that works with all appropriate caveats. That sorts out the nonsense and the claims that aren't true. Talk is super cheap. The battery

industry has to have more gibberish in it than any industry I have ever encountered. It is insane.

Books

- I had to learn how to make hardware. I had never seen a CNC machine or laid out carbon fibre. I didn't know any of these things. But if you read books and talk to experts, you will pick it up fairly quickly. It is reasonably straightforward. Just read books and talk to people, particularly books. The data rate of reading is much greater than when somebody is talking.

Booster

- Why did we name one booster Falcon and one Dragon? Falcon is named after the Millennium Falcon from Star Wars because Falcon can do the Kessel Run in seven parsecs. And the Dragon was named after "Puff the Magic Dragon" because so many people thought I must be smoking weed to do this venture.
- Falcon 1 is just our test vehicle, our first foray. It is not the end game. It is the beginning of the beginning.

Boring Company

The Boring Company began as a joke, and we decided to make it real and dig a tunnel under LA.

Boss

- If your boss is an awful person, you are going to hate coming to work.
- I try to be a decent boss most of the time, but not all the time.

Brain

- A prior track record of exceptional achievement in engineering is required but no prior experience working on the brain or human physiology is required. We will teach you what is known about the brain, which is not much, to be honest.
- In your brain you have, I think, some intrinsic elements that represent beauty and that trigger the emotion of appreciation for beauty in your mind. I think that these are relatively consistent among people. Not completely, as not everyone likes the same thing but there are many commonalities.
- If I have to allocate brain time to this one thing, then I have to take it from someone else. Well, what's that going to be? I have tried just working myself to the bone but you just can't keep doing that.

Brand

- A brand is just a perception, and perception will match reality over time. Sometimes it will be ahead, other times it will be behind. But a brand is simply a collective impression some have about a product.

Business

- Starting and growing a business is as much about the innovation, drive and determination of the people as the product they sell.
- Starting a business is not for everyone. For starting a business I'd say, the number one quality is to have a high pain threshold.

❑

California

- I was born in Africa. I came to California because it is really where new technologies can be brought to fruition, and I don't see a viable competitor.

Carbon

- Even if producing CO_2 was good for the environment, given that we are going to run out of hydrocarbons, we need to find some sustainable means of operating.
- We are playing a ridiculous game here with the atmosphere and the oceans. We are taking vast amounts of carbon from deep underground, and putting this in the atmosphere. This is senseless and ill-conceived. We should not do this.
- I don't have any fundamental dislike of hydrocarbons. I simply look at the future and say, "What is the thing that will work?" and using a non-renewable resource obviously will not work.

- It is quite surprising how little people know about geosciences, even fairly straightforward stuff like the carbon cycle. I have had conversations with quite smart and well-read people who don't understand that there is a surface carbon cycle, but if you dig stuff up from deep underground and add it to the surface carbon cycle, that fundamentally changes the chemical equilibrium of the surface of the earth. And they are surprised like, "Wow, really?"

Car Dealership

- The problem with car dealerships is you have already decided what you want to buy before you even go there, and you are just going there to talk through some annoying negotiation.

Cars

- Self-driving cars are the natural extension of active safety and something we should do.
- When Henry Ford made cheap, reliable cars, people said, 'Nah, what's wrong with a horse?' That was a huge bet he made, and it worked.
- As we go to a more autonomous future, the importance of entertainment and productivity in cars will become infinitely greater. To the degree that if you are just sitting in your car and the car is fully autonomous

and driving somewhere, the car is essentially your chauffeur.

- My opinion is it is a bridge too far to go to fully autonomous cars.
- I've predicted that within 30 years a majority of new cars made in the United States will be electric. And I don't mean hybrid, I mean fully electric.
- Nobody wants to buy a $60,000 electric Civic. But people will pay $90,000 for an electric sports car.
- I'm glad to see that BMW is bringing an electric car to market. That's cool.
- Owning a car that is not self-driving, in the long term, will be like owning a horse – you would own it and use it for sentimental reasons but not for daily use.
- Getting into a car will be like getting into an elevator – you just tell it where you want to go and it takes you there with extreme levels of safety.
- The only way a new car company breaks in is by making a car that is so compelling that people are willing to pay extra for that.
- Entertainment will be critical when cars drive themselves.

CEO

- The path to the CEO's office should not be through the CFO's office, and it should not be through the marketing department. It needs to be through the engineering and design department.

- I tried hard not to be the CEO at Tesla but I had to or it would die.
- I am Head Engineer and Chief Designer as well as CEO at SpaceX, so I don't have to cave to some money guy. I encounter CEOs who don't know the details of their technology and that is ridiculous to me.

Chance

- Don't worry about the chances of success or failure. Make sure it is possible, and then attack with full force.

Change

- Some people don't like change, they are averse to it. But you need to embrace change if the alternative is a disaster.
- I'm interested in things that change the world or that affect the future and wondrous, new technology where you see it, and you're like, "Wow, how did that even happen? How is that possible?"
- When I was in college, I wanted to be involved in things that would change the world. Now I am.
- I don't think everything needs to change the world; you know. Just say, "Is what I am doing as useful as it could be?"

- I do think it is worth thinking about whether what you are doing is going to result in a disruptive change or not. If it is just incremental, it is unlikely to be something major. It has got to be something substantially better than what is done before.
- Change is the law of life. And this is good for you. Would you like it if every day was the same? We are here to constantly enhance our experience of life and reach greater heights spiritually, physically, emotionally, and financially. When there is no progress, there is no life.

China

- I think what China is doing in the solar panel arena is awesome because they are lowering the cost of solar power for the world. They have these huge immense gigafactories that they created out in the Chinese desert with a ton of funding from the Chinese Government. So, it is like a giant donation from the Chinese Government.
- I think a good thumb rule is, "Don't compete with China with a commodity product." You are asking for trouble in that scenario.

Choice

- I think it is possible for ordinary people to choose to be extraordinary.

Coal

- It's not as though we can keep burning coal in our power plants. Coal is a finite resource, too. We must find alternatives, and it's a better idea to find alternatives sooner than wait till we run out of coal, and in the meantime, put God knows how many trillions of tons of CO_2 that used to be buried underground into the atmosphere.

College

- You don't need college to learn stuff. Everything is available, basically for free. You can learn anything you want for free; it is not a question of learning. There is a value that colleges have, which is seeing whether somebody can work hard at something, including a series of annoying homework assignments.
- Did Shakespeare go to college? Probably not.
- There is no need even to have a college degree at all or even high school.
- I think college is basically for fun and to prove that you can do your chores but it is not for learning.
- I don't consider going to college as evidence of exceptional ability. Ideally, you dropped out.
- When you go through college, you have to answer the question that the professor gives you. You don't get to say, "This is the wrong question." In reality,

you have all the degrees of freedom of reality, and so the first thing you should say is "This question is wrong."

- What is the purpose of universities at this point? I think it is mostly just to hang out with peers, have some fun, and talk to friends.

Comfort Zone

- You have to step out of your comfort zone. Be bankrupt for a while. Lose some friends. Have some sleepless nights. Most people don't get it through.

Company

- If you are trying to create a company, it's like baking a cake. You have to have all the ingredients in the right proportion.
- If you're going to create a company, the first thing you should do is create a working prototype.
- The company was bleeding money profusely, and if we didn't solve these problems in a very short time, we would die.
- Starting and growing a company is more about building a determined team than creating products or services.
- Generally people think creating companies is going to be fun. I would say it is not. It is not that fun.

There are periods of fun, and there are periods where it is just awful. Particularly if you are the CEO of the company, have a distillation of all the worst problems in the company. There is no point in spending your time on things that are going right, so you only spend your time on things that are going wrong. I think you have to feel quite compelled to do it and have a fairly high pain threshold.

- My motivation for all my companies has been to be involved in something I thought would have a significant impact on the world.
- Work hard, like every waking hour. That's the thing I would say if you are particularly starting a company.
- A company is a group organized to create a product or service, and it is only as effective as its people and how excited they are about creating. I do want to recognize a ton of super-talented people. I just happen to be the face of the companies.
- As a public company, we are subject to wild swings in our stock price that can be a major distraction for everyone working at Tesla.
- Great companies are built on great products.
- I always invest my own money in the companies that I create. I don't believe in the whole thing of just using other people's money. I don't think that's right. I am not going to ask other people to invest in something if I am not prepared to do it myself.

- I don't create companies for the sake of creating companies but to get things done.
- I don't think it is advisable to plan to sell a company.
- It is really hard to find someone who can grow a company. Running a company in a steady state is much easier than growing a company.
- The ability to attract and motivate great people is critical to the success of a company because a company is a group of people that are assembled to create a product or service. That is the purpose of a company. People sometimes forget this elementary truth. If you can get great people to join the company and work together towards a common goal or objective and have a relentless sense of perfection about that goal, then you will end up with a great product. And if you have an exceptional product, many of people will buy it, and then the company will be successful.

Competitors

- We don't think too much about what competitors are doing because I think it is important to be focused on making the best possible products. It is perhaps analogous to what they say about if you are in a race: don't worry about what the other runners are doing, just run.

- It is certainly a good compliment if all your competitors are banding together to sort of attack you, that's a good compliment. I think it is a very sincere compliment.
- In terms of our competitiveness, it mostly comes down to our pace of innovation. Our pace of innovation is much, much faster than the big aerospace companies or country-driven systems. This is generally true. If you look at innovation from large companies and smaller companies, you will notice that the smaller companies are generally better at innovating than the larger companies. It has to be that way from a Darwinian standpoint because smaller companies would just die if they didn't try innovating.

Consciousness

- I concluded that the more we can expand the scope and scale of consciousness, the better we can answer the questions or ask the questions, to understand the nature of the universe. So, therefore, we want to expand the scope and the scale of consciousness.
- From an evolutionary standpoint, human consciousness has not been around very long. A little light just went on after four and a half billion years. How often does that happen? Maybe it is quite rare.
- I hope consciousness propagates into the future and gets more sophisticated and complex and that it understands the questions to ask about the universe.

Contribution

To have your voice heard in Washington, you have to make a significant contribution.

Control

It's fine to have your eggs in one basket as long as you control what happens to that basket.

Corporation

You can think of a corporation as a cybernetic collective that is far smarter than an individual.

Creating

- When you put your blood, sweat, and tears into creating something, building something, it is like a child.
- Do more creating than you do complaining.

Critical Thinking

- Do you have the right axioms, are they relevant, and are you making the right conclusions based on those axioms? That's the essence of critical thinking, and yet it is amazing how often people fail to do that. I think wishful thinking is innate in the human brain. You want things to be the way you wish them to be, and so you tend to filter information that you shouldn't filter.

Criticism

- Constantly seek criticism. A well-thought-out critique of whatever you are doing is as valuable as gold.
- A mark of a great man lies in his response to criticism. Don't run away from criticism. Understand it. If it has some truth to it, then solve the problem, and your life or product will improve.

Customer

- Sometimes the customer doesn't know what they need.

Cyborg

- We are already cyborgs. Your phone and your computer are extensions of you, but the interface is through finger movements or speech, which are very slow.
- We are already cyborgs. You have a digital version of yourself or a partial version of yourself online in the form of your e-mails and your social media and all the things that you do. And you have, basically superpowers with your computer and your phone and the applications that are there. You have more power than the President of the United States had 20 years ago. You can answer any question; you can video conference with anyone anywhere; you can send a message to millions of people instantly. You just do incredible things.

❑

Death

- I think frankly, it is probably a good thing that we do eventually die. You know, there is a saying in physics—even physicists, who are generally quite objective—there is a saying that all physicists don't change their mind, they just die. So, maybe, you know, it's good to have this life cycle.
- Nowadays when somebody dies, they still have their electronic ghost left around. You know, their Instagram, Twitter, Facebook, emails, website, etc. are still there. Even when their bodies die.

Delegate

- I would love to delegate more, if at all possible. But the practical reality of it is that I cannot delegate because I can't find people to delegate it to.

Design

- If a design is taking too long, the design is wrong and not worth considering.

Different

- You shouldn't do things differently just because they are different. They need to be better.

DNA

- With DNA, you should be able to tell which genes are turned on or off. Current DNA sequencing cannot do that. The next generation of DNA sequencing needs to be able to do this. If somebody invents this, then we can start to very precisely identify cures for diseases.
- Trying to read our DNA is like trying to understand software code – with only 90 per cent of the code riddled with errors. It's very difficult in that case to understand and predict what that software code is going to do.

Dreams

- In this life, we are all creators. You can make a dent in the universe if you try hard and remain loyal to your dreams.
- It doesn't matter how much money you have. You are only as young or as old as your vision and your

dreams. If your vision is old and gloomy, you will feel low no matter how much money you have.

- Many people will panic to find a charger before their phones die. But won't panic to find a plan before their dreams die.

Duty

- I think we have a duty to maintain the light of consciousness to ensure it continues.

❑

Earth

- We must attempt to extend life beyond earth now. It is the first time in the four billion-years history of earth that it has been possible to extend life beyond earth. Before, this was not possible. How long will this window be open? It may be open for a long time, or it may be open for a short time. I think it would be wise to assume that it is open for a short time, and let us secure the future consciousness so that the light of consciousness is not extinguished.
- One should try to make the world a better place because the inverse makes no sense.
- The extension of life beyond earth is the most shattering or significant thing we can do as a species.
- I think life on earth must be about more than just solving problems. It has got to be something inspiring, even if it is vicarious.

- There have only been about a half dozen genuinely important events in the four-billion-year saga of life on earth: single-celled life, multi-celled life, differentiation into plants and animals, movement of animals from water to land, and the advent of mammals and consciousness.
- Sooner or later, we must expand life beyond our tiny blue mud ball—or go extinct.

Economy

- Some people have this absurd view that the economy is some magic horn of plenty like it just makes stuff. Let me just break it to the fools out there: If you don't make stuff, there is no stuff.

Education

- Don't confuse schooling with education. I didn't go to Harvard but people that work for me did.
- I do agree with Peter Thiel's point that a university education is often unnecessary. That is not to say it is unnecessary for everyone. You probably learn the vast majority of what you are going to learn there in the first two years, and most of it is from your classmates. Because you can always buy the textbooks and just read them. No one is stopping you from doing that. Now several companies, do want to see the completion of the degree because they are looking for someone who is going to persevere

and see it through to the end, and that is actually what is important to them. So, it depends on what somebody's goal is. If the goal is to start a company, I would say there is no point in finishing college. In my case, I had to, otherwise, I would get kicked out of the country.

- It is easier to land on Mars than to change the schooling system.
- What is education? You are downloading data and algorithms into your brain. And it is amazingly bad in conventional education. It shouldn't be like this excruciating chore. The more you can gamify the process of learning, the better.
- I hate it when people confuse education with intelligence. You can have a bachelor's degree and still be an idiot.

Electric Cars

- I was really into physics and I thought, well, we don't want to have civilization collapse if we run out of oil, and that's the only way of getting around. We won't be able to maintain civilization. We could have mass starvation and civilization would collapse. So, we have to have electric cars.
- A Prius is not a true hybrid. The current Prius is, like, 2 per cent electric. It's a gasoline car with slightly better mileage.

- I do encourage other manufacturers to bring electric cars to market. It's a good thing, and they need to bring it to market and keep iterating and improving and make better and better electric cars, and that's what will result in humanity achieving a sustainable transport future. I wish it would grow faster than it is.
- The fundamental enabling technology for electric cars is indeed lithiumion as a cell chemistry technology. In the absence of that, I don't think it is possible to make an electric car that is competitive with a gasoline car.
- I think there are more politicians in favour of electric cars than against them. There are still some that are against it, and I think the reasoning for that varies depending on the person, but in some cases, they just don't believe in climate change – they think oil will last forever.
- Electric cars are the future. There is no question about that at this point.

E-mails

- I do love e-mail. Wherever possible I try to communicate asynchronously. I'm adept at e-mail.

Emotional Nature

- Understand your emotional nature. If you need some quiet, alone or solitary time to recharge, make sure you get some every day. If you like to keep busy, always around people, do that. Do whatever works for you.

Employee

- You can't only look at what an individual employee gets done. You also have to look at how they have helped people around them get things done.

Engineering

- Science is discovering the essential truths about what exists in the universe while engineering is about creating things that never existed.

Enlightenment

- The only thing that makes sense is to strive for greater collective enlightenment.

Entrepreneurship

- Entrepreneurship is more like eating glass while staring at the abyss of death.

Entropy

- I think you should always bear in mind that entropy is not on your side.

Everything

- There's nothing—I've bought everything I want. I don't like yachts or anything; you know, I'm not a yacht person, and I've got pretty much the best plane I'd want to have.

Excuses

- Stop making those stupid excuses you tell yourself.

Experiment

- We are running the most dangerous experiment in history right now, which is to see how much carbon dioxide the atmosphere can handle before there is an environmental catastrophe.
- In the early days of aviation, there was a great deal of experimentation and a high death rate.
- The space shuttle was often used as an example of why you shouldn't even attempt to make something reusable. But one failed experiment does not invalidate the greater goal. If that was the case, we would never have had the light bulb.

❑

Factory

- The factory is the machine that builds the machine.
- The internal name for designing the machine that makes the machine is the Alien Dreadnought. At the point at which the factory looks like an alien dreadnought, then you know you have won.
- We are going to design a factory like you would design an advanced computer and, in fact, use engineers that are used to doing that and have them work on this. I have found that once you explain this to a first-rate engineer, the light bulb goes on. A lot of engineers don't realize that this is possible. They think that there is a wall—they are operating according to these invisible walls. So, we are in the process of just going through and explaining those walls don't exist.
- We have realized that the true problem, the true difficulty, and where the greatest potential is, is building the machine that makes the machine—in

other words, building the factory and thinking of the factory like a product. We don't try to create a car by ordering a bunch of things from a catalogue. We design the car the way it should be and then we, working with suppliers, make all of those individual components. There is almost nothing in a Model S that's in any other car. I think the same approach is the approach to take when building the machine maker, the factory. I think that the potential for improvement in the machine that makes the machine is a factor of 10 greater than the potential on the car side. I think it may be more than a factor of 10.

- You can create a demo version of a product, like a few cars worth of a product, with a small team in maybe three to six months. But to build the machine that builds the machine, it takes at least 100 to 1,000 times more resources and difficulty.

Failure

- A failure is a good option. If things are not failing, you are not trying hard enough.
- Failure to show up is half the battle. You have to try hard to do it and don't be afraid of failure.
- I messed up the first three launches. The first three launches failed. And fortunately, the fourth launch,

which was the last money that we had for Falcon 1—that fourth launch worked or that would have been it for SpaceX. But fate favoured us that day. So, the fourth launch worked.

- If something is important enough, you should try it. Even, if the probable outcome of it is a failure.
- When trying different things, you must have some acceptance of failure: failure must be an option. If failure is not an option, it is going to result in extremely conservative choices and you may get something even worse than a lack of innovation, things may go backwards.
- In baseball they don't let you just sit there and wait for the perfect pitch till you get a really easy one, they only give you three shorts and on the third one they say, "Okay may, get off, get someone else up there." So, you get three strikes in baseball. There is bound to be some amount of failure.
- Failure is essentially irrelevant unless it is catastrophic.
- There is a silly notion that failure is not an option at NASA. A failure is an option here. If you are not failing, you are not innovating enough.
- My mentality is that of a samurai. I would rather commit seppuku than fail.

Fear

- I wouldn't say I have a lack of fear. I would like my fear emotion to be less because it is very distracting and fries my nervous system.
- I feel fear quite strongly. But if what we are doing is important then I just override the fear.
- Fear is problematic to deal with. I feel it quite strongly. If I think something is important enough, I'll make myself do it despite fear. But it can sap the will. I hate fear; I wish I had it less.
- Something that can be helpful is fatalism, to some degree. If you accept the probabilities, then that diminishes fear.
- Drive overrides fear, but I feel the fear.
- Fear is raw, human emotion. Everyone feels it. What matters is whether you run away from it and take a blow to your confidence, or you face it, understand it and then defeat it to strengthen your confidence.
- Don't be afraid of new arenas.
- I wouldn't say I am fearless. I think I feel fear quite strongly.

Feedback

- Pay attention to negative feedback, and solicit it, particularly from friends because they will be thinking about it but they won't tell you.

- I think it is very important to have a feedback loop, where you are constantly thinking about what you have done and how you could be doing it better. I think that is the single best piece of advice: constantly think about how you could be doing things better and question yourself.
- You want to be extra rigorous about making the best possible thing you can. Find everything that is wrong with it and fix it. Seek negative feedback, particularly from friends.
- I have no problem with negative feedback, nor do I have a problem with critical reviews. If I had a problem with critical reviews, I would spend all my time battling critical reviews. There have been hundreds of negative articles and yet I have only spoken out a few times. I don't have a problem with critical reviews, I have a problem with false reviews.
- I also believe in having a tight feedback loop between engineering and production. If production is far away or distantly removed from engineering, you lose that feedback loop. Someone who designed the car in a particular way doesn't realize that it is very difficult to manufacture in the particular way that it is designed. But if the factory floor is 50 feet away from their desk, then they can go out and they can just see it. It is obvious. And they can have a dialogue

with the people on the floor. Likewise, many of the people on the manufacturing team have fantastic ideas about how to improve the car, but if they are far away, they can't communicate that to the engineers who designed it. I think that it is often neglected, but having that strong bidirectional feedback loop between engineering and production helps make the car better, find efficiencies, and lower the cost.

Finish Line

- The finish line is usually much further away than you think.

Flying Cars

- We could make a flying car, but that's not the hard part. The hard part is 'how do you make a flying car that's super safe and quiet?' Because, if it is a howler, you are going to make people very unhappy.
- Flying cars sound cool, but then they do make a lot of wind, they are quite noisy, and the probability of something falling on your head is much higher.
- Let's just say that if something is flying over your head, a whole bunch of flying cars going all over the place, that is not an anxiety-reducing situation. You don't think to yourself, "Well, I feel better about today." You are thinking, "Did they service their

hubcap, or is it going to come off and guillotine me?" things like that.

Focus

- Focus on signal over noise; don't waste time on stuff that doesn't improve the situation.
- Focus on 3-5 years down the line. Most people don't realize that the life they live right now is based solely on decisions they made 3-5 years ago.
- Focus is incredibly important. If you have a certain number of resources, to the degree that you diffuse your focus, you impede your ability to execute.

Fuel Cells

- The fuel cell is just a fundamentally inferior way of delivering electrical energy to an electric motor than batteries.

Fuels

- Bio-fuels such as ethanol require enormous amounts of cropland and end up displacing either food crops or natural wilderness, neither of which is feasible.
- Every gasoline or diesel car that is going down the road has a de facto subsidy on it. People sometimes don't appreciate that. Whenever something is burning fossil fuels, it has a de facto subsidy. It is a subsidy for the public good. They are spending

the carbon capacity of the oceans and atmosphere, not to mention the sulphur and nitrous oxides that are emitted, as it turns out, in greater quantities than regulators were told.

Fundamentals

- Start with the basics and build from there. You can't master something by overlooking the fundamentals.

Future

- If you wake up in the morning and think the future is going to be better, it is a bright day. Otherwise, it's not.
- I like to die thinking that humanity has a bright future. If we can solve sustainable energy and be well on our way to becoming a multi-planetary species with a self-sustaining civilization on another planet, I think that would be good.
- There is a fundamental difference, if you sort of look into the future, between a humanity that is a space-faring civilization, that's out there exploring the stars compared with one where we are forever confined to earth until some eventual extinction event.
- The value of beauty and inspiration is greatly underrated, no question there. But I want to make it clear; I am not trying to be anyone's saviour. I am

just trying to think about the future and not be sad or pessimistic.

- You must be willing to lose it all but be willing to keep going into the future.
- The future will be weird.
- In the future, we will look—and my future here, I am talking about the end of the century—we will look back on gasoline-powered cars the same way we look back on coal; as a sort of quaint anachronism that is in a museum.
- In future, the real issue will be an ageing and declining world population by 2050, not overpopulation.
- I look at the future from a standpoint of probabilities. It is like a branching stream of probabilities, and there are actions that we can take that affect those probabilities or that accelerate one thing or slow down another thing.
- The world's population is accelerating towards collapse but few seem to notice or care.
- I think fundamentally the future is vastly more exciting and interesting if we are a space-faring civilization and a multi-planet species than if we are not. You want to be inspired by things. You want to wake up in the morning and think the future is going to be tremendous. And that's what being a space-faring civilization is all about. It is about believing in the future and thinking that the future will be better

than the past. And I can't think of anything more exciting than going out there and being among the stars.

- The future of humanity is going to bifurcate in two directions: Either it's going to become multi-planetary, or it's going to remain confined to one planet and eventually, there is going to be an extinction event.
- The thing that drives me is that I want to be able to think about the future and feel contented about that. Do what we can to have the future be as fulfilling as possible, to be inspired by what is likely to happen, and to look forward to the next day.
- I read a lot of science fiction as a child and tried to think about the future and the problems that needed to be solved to make it a bright future, and I tried to get involved in that.
- I think it is important to have a future that is inspiring, gratifying and appealing. I just think there have to be reasons that you wake up in the morning and you want to live. Why do you want to live? What's the point? What inspires you? What do you love about the future? And if we are not out there, if the future does not include being out there among the stars and being a multi-planet species, I find that it is incredibly depressing if that is not the future that we are going to have.

- What I am trying to do is to minimize future essential threats or take whatever action I can to ensure the future is bright.
- You want to have a future where you're expecting things to be better, not one where you're expecting things to be worse.
- Going from PayPal, I thought, "Well, what are some of the other problems that are likely to most affect the future of humanity?" Not from the perspective, "What's the best way to make money?"

❑

“G

Goals

- People work better when they know what the goal is and why. People must look forward to coming to work in the morning and enjoy working.
- Honestly, I am just trying to do the most amount of good with the time that I have on this earth. And, you know, not always succeeding, but that’s the goal.
- If you give yourself 30 days to clean your home, it will take 30 days. If you give yourself 3 hours, it will take 3 hours. The same applies to your goals, plans and ambitions.
- We should create goals that matter to us. What is the one thing you would change about the world? Go work on it, do it, be it, achieve it.

God

- I am the punishment of God. If you had not committed great sins, God wouldn’t have sent a punishment like I upon you.

Government

- Government isn't that good at the rapid advancement of technology. It tends to be better at funding basic research. To have things take off, you should have commercial companies do it.
- Government is simply the largest corporation. It is the ultimate corporation.
- I don't think the government intends to stand in the way of innovation, but sometimes they can overregulate industries to the point where innovation becomes very difficult. The auto industry used to be a superb hotbed of innovation at the beginning of the twentieth century, but now there are so many regulations.
- At the end of the day, governments respond to popular pressure. If you tell politicians that your vote depends on them doing the right thing with climate change, then that makes a difference. If they are having a fundraising event or a dinner party and if somebody is asking them, "Hey, what are you doing about the climate?" then they will take action. I think you have tremendous power. You have the power to make the change.
- The goal of government should be to maximize the happiness of the people. Giving money to each person allows them to decide what meets their needs,

rather than the blunt tool of legislation, which creates self-serving special interests.

- I am generally a fan of minimal government interference in the economy. The government should be the referee but not the player, and there shouldn't be too many referees. But there is an exception, which is when there's an unpriced externality such as the CO_2 capacity of the oceans and atmosphere. When you have an unpriced externality, then the normal market mechanisms do not work, and then it is the government's role to intervene sensibly. The best way to intervene is to assign a proper price to whatever the common good is that is being consumed.

Grades

- It shouldn't be that you have got these grades where people move in lockstep and everyone goes through English, Mathematics, Science, and so forth from fifth grade to sixth grade to seventh grade as if it is an assembly line. People are not objects on an assembly line. That is a ridiculous notion. People learn and are interested in different things at different places. You want to disconnect the whole grade-level aspect from the subjects. Allow people to progress at the fastest pace that they can or are interested in, in each subject. It seems like a really obvious thing.

❑

Habits

- Reading 20 pages per day is reading 30 books per year. Saving $10 per day is $3,650 per year. Running I mile per day is 365 miles per year. Becoming 1 per cent better per day is 37x better per year. Small habits are underestimated.

Happen

- We are going to make it happen. As God is my bloody witness, I'm hell-bent on making it work.
- I could either watch it happen or be a part of it.
- I say something, and then it usually happens. Maybe not on schedule, but it usually happens.
- You have to be fairly driven to make it happen. Otherwise, you will just make yourself miserable.

High Intensity

- The idea of lying on a beach as my main thing just sounds like the worst. It sounds horrible to me. I would go mad. I would have to be on serious drugs. I'd be super-duper bored. I like high intensity.

History

- If anyone thinks they would rather be in a different part of history, they are probably not an astute student of history. Life sucked in the old days. People knew very little, and you were likely to die at a young age of some horrible disease. You would probably have no teeth by now. It would be particularly awful if you were a woman.
- The lessons of history would suggest that civilizations move in cycles. You can track that back quite far—the Babylonians, the Sumerians, followed by the Egyptians, the Romans, Chinese. We're obviously in a very upward cycle right now, and hopefully, that remains the case. But it may not.

Humanity

- It doesn't do a great deal to advance the goal of humanity. I would pay a million not to spend six months in Russia. And besides this, my interest is how we enable many other people to go to space, not necessarily me, personally.
- I want to make rockets 100 times, if not 1,000 times better. The ultimate objective is to make humanity a multi-planet species. Thirty years from now, there

will be a base on the moon and Mars, and people will travel back and forth on SpaceX rockets.

- Creating a neural lace is the thing that matters for humanity to achieve symbiosis with machines.
- If humanity is to become multi-planetary, the fundamental breakthrough that needs to occur in rocketry is a rapidly and completely reusable rocket achieving it would be on a par with what the Wright brothers did.
- For me, it was never about money, but about solving problems for the future of humanity.
- The probable life span of human civilization is much greater if we are a multi-planet species as opposed to a single-planet species. If we are a single-planet species, then eventually there will be some extinction event, either from humans or some natural phenomenon.

❑

Ideas

- Good ideas are always crazy until they are not.
- People will reject your ideas even when they care for you. So, discover the truths on your own and trust your gut.
- I have a million ideas. There is no shortage of that.

Imagination

- You people are the magicians of the twenty-first century. Don't let anything hold you back. Imagination is the limit. Go out there and create some magic.

Important

- I am not saying we will become multi-planetary for sure. The odds are we won't succeed. But when something is important enough, then you should do it even if the odds are not in your favour.
- I think the things that we think are crucial now will probably not be important in the future.

Impossible

- Many things are improbable, and only a few are impossible.

Innovation

- When somebody has a breakthrough innovation, it is rarely one little thing. Very rarely, is it one little thing? It's usually a whole bunch of things that collectively amount to a huge innovation.
- Establish an expectation of innovation, and the compensation structure must reflect that. There must also be an allowance for failure because if you try something new, necessarily there is some chance it will not work. If you punish people too much for failure, then they will respond accordingly, and the innovation you get will be very incrementalist. Nobody is going to try anything bold for fear of getting fired or being punished in some way. The risk-reward must be balanced and favour taking bold moves. Otherwise, it will not happen.
- There is an extreme lack of innovation in large industries. I saw it as an opportunity.
- There is a lot of innovation going on. There are probably a few too many talented entrepreneurs in the internet space, and I think their talent actually would be better served in some other industries. But I don't think we are facing some sort of low innovation period.

- The private sector is very good at organization and innovation.
- It is important to create an environment that fosters innovation, but you want to let it evolve in a Darwinian way. You don't want to, at a high level, at a gut level, pick a technology and decide it may not be. You should let things evolve.
- In certain sectors, like automotive, solar and space, you don't see new entrants. There is not a lot of capital going to start-ups and not many entrepreneurs going into these arenas. The problem is that in the absence of new entrants into an industry, you don't have that force for innovation. It is the new entrants that drive innovation more than anything. That is why I have devoted my efforts to those industries, and they are industries that require considerable capital to get going.

Inspire

- If you need inspiring words, don't do it.
- You don't always improve but you can aspire to improve. You can aspire to be less wrong.

Intelligence

- Over time I think we will probably see a closer merger of biological and digital intelligence. It is mostly about the bandwidth, the speed of the connection between your brain and the digital version of yourself, particularly the output.

- I think we need to think of intelligence as really not being uniquely confined to humans. And that the potential for intelligence in computers is far greater than in biology.

Internet

- I think most of the important stuff on the Internet has been built. There will be continued innovation, for sure, but the great problems of the Internet have essentially been solved.
- The only reason I started an internet company back in 1995, was because there were only a few internet companies and I couldn't get a job at any of them.
- The most remarkable thing that we do have today is the internet and access to all the world's information from anywhere. Having a supercomputer in your pocket is, I think, something people wouldn't have predicted in 'Back to the Future'.

Interns

- Interns are fantastic because they don't know what's impossible.

Investment

- I am not an investor. So many people think I invest in things. I don't invest in anything.

- I am an ardent believer in 'don't ask investors to invest their money if you are not prepared to invest your money'. I believe in the opposite philosophy of other people's money. It just doesn't seem right to me that if you ask other people to invest that you shouldn't also invest. I would rather lose my money than any of my friends' money or investors' money.

❑

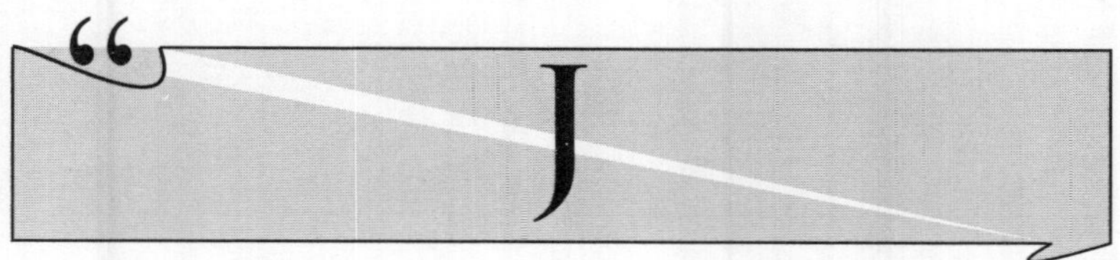

Justice System

- I have immense respect for the justice system. So far, I have found judges to be adept at justice.

❑

Kids

- When I was, I don't know, five or six or something, I thought that I was insane because it was clear to me that the minds of other people weren't exploding with ideas all the time.
- When I was a child, I would just walk around reading books all the time. And I was also the youngest child in my grade, so I was quite small. I was a sort of smart aleck and a recipe for disaster. I would get called every name in the book and beaten up.
- I usually describe myself as an engineer; that's basically what I've been doing since I was a youngster.
- Children have a wonderful way of living one moment at a time. Their feelings are often based on events as they happen. They are mostly joyful. At times, they may feel negative and this usually happens in a fight over toys or games. However, as soon as they get distracted by something new, they no longer hold on

to their negative emotions. Instead, they are happy once again. As adults, we tend to remain angry or upset even way after the event. We are experts in accumulating anger in an internal storehouse. Our minds get stuck interminably in the past. We do not live in the present moment as it is now. It is hard to be happy or cheerful when we have no present-moment awareness.

- My background educationally is physics and economics, and I grew up in an engineering environment – my father is an electromechanical engineer. And so, there were many engineering things around me.
- When I was a little kid, I was really scared of the dark. But then I came to know, dark just means the absence of photons in the visible wavelength – 400 to 700 nanometres. Then I thought, well it is really to be afraid of a lack of photons. Then I wasn't afraid of the dark anymore after that.
- When I was little, I would just question everything. It would infuriate my parents that I wouldn't just believe them when they said something because I'd ask them why. And then I'd consider whether that response made sense given everything else I knew.
- I always try to reserve time for my children because I love hanging out with them. The children are great.

I mean, 99 per cent of the time, they make you happier. Of anything in my life, I would say kids by far make me the happiest. Often, children are in their own worlds. They don't want to talk to their father for hours on end, generally. So, I can be in the same room with them, and they can talk to me from time to time, but I can get some e-mails done, get some work done, and then whenever they want to talk to me, they can.

- There are things you look for: You have to look forward in the morning to do your work. You do want to have a significant financial reward. And you want to have a possible effect on the world. If you can find all three, then you have something that you can tell your children.

Knowledge

- View knowledge as sort of a semantic tree. Make sure you understand the fundamental principles like the trunk and big branches before you get into the leaves/details or there is nothing for them to hang on to.

❑

Laws

- Laws of Thermodynamics:

  1. You can't win.
  2. You can't break even.
  3. You can't stop playing.

- I think we need to take a look at our immigration laws. If there are talented people doing graduate courses in engineering at our universities, we don't want to send them home. We should do everything we can to keep them here. For every person who is an ace engineer, there are probably 10 jobs that will be created if that person stays here. It is an enormous multiplier effect.

Leaders

- Here in the West, people often don't like listening to their leaders, even if they are right.

Life

- Life is too short for long-term grudges.
- To speak for myself, I would rather eat delectable food and live a shorter life. To be frank, I wouldn't exercise at all if I could.
- Life has to be about more than just solving problems.
- Life can't just be about solving one miserable problem after another—that can't be the only thing. There need to be things that inspire you, that make you glad to wake up in the morning and be part of humanity.
- Use the weekend to build the life you want instead of trying to escape the life you have. You are not going to hit your goals or achieve your objectives by getting drunk and partying every weekend. Work hard now so your future self will thank you.
- Life is so much simpler when you stop explaining yourself to people and just do what works for you.
- And we need things in life that are exciting and inspiring. It can't just be about solving some awful problem. There have to be reasons to wake up in the morning and want to live.

Like

- Don't tell me what you like, tell me what you don't like.

- Whatever area you get into you, given that even if you are the very best, there is always a chance of failure. So, I think it's important that you like what you are doing.

Love

- We need to figure out how to have the things we love, and not destroy the world.
- If I'm not in love, if I'm not with a long-term companion, I cannot be happy.
- This may sound odd, but love is the answer.

❑

M

Man

- Man has the power to act as his destroyer – and that is the way he has acted throughout most of his history
- You are already symbiotic AI or computers. It is just a question of your data rate. The communication speed between your phone and your brain is slow.
- An asteroid or a super-volcano could certainly destroy us, but we also face risks the dinosaurs never saw: An engineered virus, nuclear war, inadvertent creation of a micro black hole, or some as-yet-unknown technology could spell the end of us.
- We are the first species capable of self-annihilation.
- We are all chimps. We are one notch above a chimp.

Magic

- I read a quote from Arthur C. Clark that said 'Sufficiently advance technology is indistinguishable from magic.' And that's true. If you go back say 300 years, the things we take for granted today you would be burned at the stake for. You know, being able to fly, that's crazy. Being able to see over long distances. Being able to communicate, having effectively with the internet a group mind of sorts. And having access to all the world's information instantly from almost anywhere on the earth. This is stuff that really would be magic. It would be considered magic in times past.

Manufacture

- Manufacturing used to be highly valued in the United States, and these days it is not, it is often looked down upon, which I think is wrong.
- Manufacturing is insanely difficult. It is underappreciated in its difficulty.

Mars

- I think if you are going to choose a place to die, then Mars is probably not a bad choice.
- I was trying to figure out why we had not sent any people to Mars because the obvious next step after Apollo was to send people to Mars. I discovered that NASA had no plans to send people to Mars or even back to the Moon.
- There are many people worrying about life contamination on Mars, but anything that can survive on Mars is so tough, that it's insane. It is cold and

there's a lot of UV radiation, and it is not going to be too worried about anything we end from earth.

- Does it make sense for me to spend time designing and building a house? Or should I be allocating that time to getting us to Mars? I should probably do the latter. What's more important, Mars or a house? I like Mars.
- Mars is the only place in the solar system where life can become multi-planetary.
- Land on Mars, a round-trip ticket – half a million dollars. It can be done. You can only go there every two years because the orbital synchronization of earth and Mars is about every two years. But I think it would be an interesting way for civilization to develop. People would meet each other and be like, "What orbital synchronization did you arrive on?"
- You need to live in a dome initially, but over time you could terraform Mars to look like earth and eventually walk around outside without anything on. So, it's a fixer-upper of a planet.
- You are not going to create revolutionary cars or rockets 40 hours a week. It just won't work. Colonizing Mars isn't going to happen 40 hours a week.
- The pace of progress on Mars depends on the pace of progress of SpaceX.

- It was obvious to me that we could never colonize Mars without reusability, any more than America would have been colonized if they had to burn the ships after every trip.
- The quick way is to drop thermonuclear weapons over the poles to warm Mars up to make it hospitable for humans.
- If humanity doesn't land on Mars in my lifetime, I would be very disappointed.
- I think the first journeys to Mars are going to be very dangerous. The risk of fatality will be high—there is just no way around it. I would not suggest sending children. It would be, basically 'are you ready to die?' situation. If that is fine with you, then you are a candidate for going.
- You could warm Mars up, over time, with greenhouse gases.
- I would like to die on Mars. Just not on impact.

MBAs

- I think that there might be too many MBAs running companies.
- As much as possible, avoid hiring MBAs. MBA programmes don't teach people how to create companies.

- I would much rather promote someone who has strong engineering ability than so-called management ability. We do hire some MBAs but it is usually despite the MBA, not because of it.

Media

- Sometimes the media tries to create a more antagonistic position that is the case.

Mind

- Discover, what your mind is drawn to – movies, painting, singing, writing, engineering, rapping. Pick whatever naturally comes to mind. Work on it for a few months, don't dismiss it outwardly. Then when you have built some skill, take it to the professional level.
- What makes innovative thinking happen? I think it's a mindset. You have to decide.

Money

- Money, in my view, is essentially an information system for label allocation, so it has no power in and of itself; it is like a database for guiding people as to what they should do.

Multi-Planetary

- If we are going to have any chance of sending stuff

to other star systems, we need to be laser-focused on becoming a multi-planet civilization.

- You want multiple companies competing to advance the future of spaceflight so we can ultimately become a multi-planet species in a space-fearing civilization.
- If we continue with the Apollo programme and get to Mars and beyond then that will seem far more important in the historical context than anything else we do today. The day multi-planetary species came about in existence, the things like the Soviet Union will be forgotten or merely remembered by arcane historical scholars. Things like the invasion of Iraq won't even be a footnote.
- From a resource standpoint, I am talking about less than one per cent of earth's resources should be dedicated to making multi-planetary or making consciousness multi-planetary. I think it should be somewhere in between how much we spend on lipstick and how much we spend on healthcare.

❑

Naysayers

➢ What I found ironic about many of the naysayers is that the very people will transition from saying it was impossible to say it was obvious. And I am like, "Wait a second. Was it obvious or impossible? It can't be both."

Neuralink

➢ From a long-term existential standpoint, the purpose of Neuralink is to create a high-bandwidth interface to the brain, to such an extent that we can be symbiotic AI.

News

➢ We can't have like willy-nilly proliferation of fake news, that's unreasonable. You can't have more types of fake news than real news. That's allowing public deception to go unchecked. That's not feasible.

❑

Optimism

- I always have optimism but I am realistic. It was not with the expectation of great success that I started Tesla or SpaceX. It's just that I thought they were important enough to do anyway.
- Creating a personal and professional culture of optimism and vision is essential for any dynamic and innovative organization.
- I would rather be optimistic and wrong than pessimistic and right.
- I'm reasonably optimistic about the future, especially the future of the United States – for the century, at least.

❑

Passion

- People should pursue what they are passionate about. That will make them happier than pretty much anything else.

Patience

- Patience is a virtue, and I'm learning patience. It's a tough lesson. Patience is required because life doesn't change overnight. So be patient, take it one day at a time.
- Stop being patient and start asking yourself, "how do I accomplish my 10-year plan in 6 months?" you will probably fail but you will be a lot further along than the other person who simply accepted it was going to take 10 years.

People

- I would tell my people that they will get to see their families more often when we go bankrupt.

- I think people should be more amiable and genial to each other and give more credit to others and don't assume that they are mean until they know they are mean. It is easy to demonize people; you are usually wrong about it. People are more pleasant than you think.
- You need people who lift your spirits, not the ones who drain your energy and make you want to curl up in your bed.
- If you try to convince the public to do something, you have to think, "All right, how is this going to read? What message are we going to try to convey? What will people respond to? What would I respond to if I am an objective member of the public?" If you are trying to change people's mind or get people to be enthusiastic about something, then you have to think, "OK, what's that message? What's going to get them excited?"
- A small group of very technically strong people will always beat a large group of moderately strong people.
- Whenever there is something that affects the public good, then there does need to be some form of public oversight.
- Every person in your company is a vector. The sum of all vectors determines your progress.

- The only reason I was able to accomplish things is the talented people willing to work with me.
- Frankly, I think most people can learn a lot more than they think they can. They sell themselves short without trying.
- Getting the right people is extremely important. And I interview everyone at SpaceX personally. And we are a 500-person company. So that's several interviews.
- Some of the happiest-seeming most cheerful people are some of the saddest people in reality.
- When people understand it's done or dies and if we work hard, persevere and pull through, it's going to be a marvellous outcome; people will give it everything they've got.

Persistence

- Persistence is very important. You should not give up unless you are forced to give up.
- No, I don't ever give up. I would have to be dead or completely incapacitated.

Physics

- I tend to approach things from a physics framework. And physics teaches you to reason from first principles rather than by analogy.

- Physics is figuring out how to discover new things that are counterintuitive, like quantum mechanics. It's counterintuitive.
- Physics is an excellent framework for thinking. Boil things down to their fundamental truths and reason or ratiocinate from there.
- It is interesting to think of physics as a set of compression algorithms for the universe. That's basically what formulas are.
- I do think a solid and sound framework for thinking in physics, you know, the first principles of reasoning. What I mean by that is to boil things down to their fundamental truths and reason from there as opposed to reasoning by analogy. Throughout most of our life, we get through life by reasoning by analogy, which essentially means copying what other people do with slight variations. And you have to do that, otherwise mentally you wouldn't be able to get through the day. But when you want to do something new, you have to apply the physics approach. Physics has figured out how to discover new things that are counterintuitive, like quantum mechanics; it is counterintuitive.
- I try to be hyper-rational. So, if the reasoning fits, and you are not violating the laws of physics or something, then that's the thing you should do.

Planet

- As you heat the planet, it's just like boiling a pot.
- It has always been my belief that it is our destiny to go beyond our planet and develop sustainable environments elsewhere.

Politics or Politicians

- I wish politicians were better at science.
- You know, I am socially very liberal and then economically right of centre, or centre. I don't know. I am not a communist.

Possible

- The first step is to establish that something is possible; then the probability will occur.

Predicting

- The tricky thing with predicting things midway through an exponential is that if things double every year, or even just grow 50 per cent, then if you shift plus-minus one year, it has a massive or colossal effect on the number.

Price

- The reality is gas prices should be much more expensive than they are because we are not incorporating the true damage to the environment and the hidden costs of mining oil and transporting it to the US. Whenever you have an unpriced externality, you have a slight market failure, to the degree that eternality remains unpriced.

Problems

- I don't spend my time pontificating about high-concept issues; I spend my time-solving engineering and manufacturing problems.
- When you struggle with a problem that is when you understand it.
- When I interview people, I just ask them to tell me the story of their career and some of the tougher problems that they have dealt with, how they coped with those, and how they made decisions at key transition points. Usually, that is enough for me to get an instinctive gut feeling about someone, and what I am looking for is evidence of exceptional ability. Did they face really difficult problems and overcome them? Usually, the person who had to struggle with the problem understands it and they don't forget if it was very difficult. You can ask them very detailed questions about it, and they will know the answer, whereas the person who was not truly responsible for the accomplishment will not know the details.

Process

- I don't believe in a process. When I interview a potential employee and he/she says that 'it's all about the process,' I see that as a bad or negative sign. The problem is that at many big companies, the process becomes a substitute for thinking. You are encouraged to behave like a minuscule gear in a complex machine. Frankly, it allows you to keep people who aren't that smart or that creative.

Product

- I do think there is immense potential if you have a compelling product and people are willing to pay a premium for that. I think that is what Apple has shown. You can buy a much cheaper cell phone or laptop but Apple's products are so much better than the alternative, and people are willing to pay that premium.
- It is not about the product you create; it is how you create it. If you create an acceptable product and then stop working hard, your customers will soon be taken by companies who focus on innovation and improving their customer experience.
- There should be more focus on the product or service itself, and less focus on board meetings and finances.

- It is quite difficult to create an integrated product if you are forced to be at an arm's length and be two different companies. If we give a special deal to SolarCity, and SolarCity is not a part of Tesla, then why are we doing that? We can do that if SolarCity is part of Tesla; we can't do it if SolarCity is a separate company.
- Fundamentally, if you don't have a compelling product at a compelling price, you don't have a great company.
- When it is a radically new product, people don't know that they want it because it is not in their scope. When they first started making TVs, they did a nationwide survey, I think this might have been in 1946 or 1948, they asked people, "Will you ever buy a TV?" and 96 per cent of respondents said, "No."
- How does this wealth arise? If you organize people in a better way to produce products and services that are better than what existed before and you have some ownership in that company, then that essentially gives you the right to allocate more capital.
- Any product that needs a manual to work is broken.
- If you are entering anything where there is an existing marketplace, against large, entrenched competitors,

then your product or service needs to be much better than theirs. It can't be slightly better, because then you put yourself in the shoes of the consumer, you are always going to buy the trusted brand unless there is a major difference.

Productivity

- For a company, when it is very small, productivity grows quickly because of the specialization of labour. Then productivity per person declines due to communication issues as the company grows bigger. As you have more and more increasing layers through which communication has to flow, that necessarily imparts errors. Every time information flows from one person to another, even with the best of intentions, you have information loss to the degree that you can alleviate that by doing things like skip-level meetings, I think it's a worthwhile idea.

Profit

- I think the profit motive is a sound one if the rules of industry are properly set up. There is nothing fundamentally wrong with profit. Profit just means that people are paying you more for whatever you are doing than you are spending to create it. That's a good thing.

Progress

- If we could do high-speed rail in California just half a notch above what they've done on the Shanghai line in China, and if we had a straight path from Los Angeles to San Francisco, as well as the milk run, at least that would progress.
- If we don't improve our pace of progress, I am going to be dead before we go to Mars. I would like to be alive by the time we go to Mars.

Purpose

- A strong sense of purpose makes you persevere when things get tough.
- Many children are in school puzzled as to why they are there. I think if you can explain the 'why' of things, then that makes an appreciable difference in people's motivation. Then they understand the purpose.

Push

- Push yourself because no one else is going to do it for you.

❑

Questions

- The tough thing is figuring out what questions to ask, but once you do that, the rest is really easy.
- Start somewhere and then be prepared to question your assumptions, fix what you did wrong and adapt to reality.

❑

Radical Breakthroughs

- If you don't push for radical breakthroughs, you are not going to get radical outcomes.

Redwood

- If you want to grow a giant redwood, you need to ensure the seeds are fine, nurture the sapling, and work out what might potentially stop it from growing all the way along. Anything that breaks it at any point stops that growth.

Republican

- I'm personally a moderate and a registered independent, so I'm not strongly Democratic or strongly Republican.

Resourcefulness

- My advice to people is to be useful to others. It is very difficult to be useful to others. To do a genuinely useful thing for others is what we should all be trying to do. It is very difficult.

- Many people derive their meaning from their employment, so if you are not needed, if there is not a need for your labour, what is the meaning? Do you have meaning? Do you feel useless?

Retire

- I just want to retire before I become senile because if I don't retire before I go senile, then I'll do more damage than good at that point.

Risk

- As you get older, your obligations increase. And once you have a family, you start taking risks not just for yourself but for your family as well. It gets much harder to do things that might not work out. So now is the time to do that—before you have those obligations. I encourage you to take risks now and do something bold. You won't regret it.
- The risk is handsomely rewarded in the business world.
- There's a tremendous bias against taking risks. Everyone is trying to optimize their security-covering.
- Don't be afraid of taking risks as long as you take calculated risks. Understand the consequences

clearly and learn from people who have walked the same path earlier.

- Things you know early in life, I did several of risky things when I didn't have so much that depended on me. Now, I have to be more cautious about risky things.

Road to Hell

- "The road to hell is paved with good intentions." I mean, it is mostly paved with bad intentions but there are some good-intentions paving stones in there too.

Rockets

- The rockets are cool. There's no getting around that.
- The revolutionary breakthrough will come with rockets that are fully and rapidly reusable. We will never conquer Mars unless we do that. It will be too expensive. The American colonies would never have been pioneered if the ships that crossed the ocean hadn't been reusable.
- I concluded that there wasn't a plausible reason for rockets to be so expensive and that they could be much less. Even in an expendable format, they could be less, and if one could make them reusable, like aeroplanes, then the cost of rocketry and space travel would drop dramatically.

- We are advancing the technology of launch by having reusable rockets. Reusability has been important for access to space. It is somewhat insane to have a rocket to be expendable.
- There are many more ways to fail than to succeed. Particularly for a rocket, there are a thousand ways the thing can fail and one way it can work. You could have a lot of rocket failures to explore how it could fail. But I do think that one great thing about Silicon Valley is that failure is not a big stigma. It is like if you can try hard and it doesn't work out, that's all right. You can learn from that and do another company, and it is not a big deal.
- I had so many people try to talk me out of starting a rocket company, it was absurd.
- My vision is for a fully reusable rocket transport system between earth and Mars that can re-fuel on Mars—this is very important—so you don't have to carry the return fuel when you go there. If you had to buy a new plane each time you flew somewhere, it would be incredibly expensive.
- The odds of me coming into the rocket business, not knowing anything about rockets, not having ever built anything, I mean, I would have to be insane if I thought the odds were in my favour.
- You need to be in the position where it is the cost of

the fuel that matters and not the cost of building the rocket in the first place.

- Boeing just took $20 billion and 10 years to improve the efficiency of their planes by 10 per cent. That's pretty lame. I have a design in mind for a vertical lift-off supersonic jet that would be a vast improvement.
- Initially, when I told people I was trying to create a rocket company, they thought I was crazy. That seemed like a most improbable thing. And I agreed with them; I think it was improbable but sometimes the improbable happens.
- I think all modes of transport will become fully electric, with the ironic exception of rockets. There is just no way around Newton's third law.
- It is absurd that we build these sophisticated rockets and then crash them every time we fly. This is mad. So yes, I can't emphasize how profound this is and how important reusability is. Often, I will be told, "But you could get more pay-load if you made it expendable." I said yes, you could also get more pay-load from an aircraft if you get rid of the landing gear and the flaps and just parachute out when you got to your destination. But that would be ludicrous and you would sell zero aircraft. So, reusability is fundamental.
- When people ask me why I started a rocket company,

I say, "I was trying to learn how to turn a large fortune into a small one."

- In the case of spaceflight, the critical breakthrough that is necessary for spaceflight is the rapid and complete reusability of rockets, just as we have for aircraft. We can imagine that if an aircraft was single-use almost no one would fly. You can buy, say, a 747, it might be 250 or 300 million dollars or something like that and you would need two of them for a round-trip. Nobody is going to pay a million dollars for a ticket to fly. Since you can reuse the aircraft tens of thousands of times, air travel becomes much more affordable. The same is true for rockets.
- The speed of a rocket is always going to be roughly the same. The convenience and comfort are going to be about the same. Reliability has to be at least as good as what's been done before. Otherwise, people won't use your rockets to launch a hundred-million-dollar satellites. Though, there is not going to be much improvement there. So, you are left with one key parameter against which technology improvements must be judged and that is cost.
- I said, "All right, let's look at the first principles. What is a rocket made up of? It is made up of aerospace-grade aluminium alloys, plus some titanium, copper and carbon fibre." And then I asked, "What is the

value of those materials on the commodity market?" It turned out that the materials cost of a rocket was around 2 per cent of the typical price; which is an unbelievable ratio for a large mechanical product.

Rules

- If the rules are such that you can't make progress, then you have to fight the rules.
- The basic rule for meetings is that unless somebody is getting enormous value from the information they are receiving or they are contributing to the meeting itself, they should not be there. And we also have a rule that if somebody is in a meeting and finds that this meeting is not helping them in a meaningful way and they are not contributing to the meeting, they should just leave.
- Rules and regulations are immortal. And if we keep making more every year, and do not do something about removing them, then eventually we will be able to do nothing.

❑

Scepticism

- One should have a healthy scepticism of things in general, and from a scientific standpoint, you always look at things probabilistically, not definitively. Often, if somebody is a sceptic in the science community, what they are saying is that they are not sure that it is 100 per cent certain that this is the case.

School

- You can learn whatever you need to do to start a successful business either in school or out of school. A school, in theory, should help accelerate that process, and I think oftentimes it does. It can be an efficient learning process, perhaps more efficient than empirically learning lessons. There are examples of successful entrepreneurs who never graduated from high school, and there are those that have PhDs. I think the important principle is to be dedicated to learning what you need to know, whether that is in school or empirically.

Service

- The best way to experience service is, of course, not to experience service.
- I have made it a principle within Tesla that we should never attempt to make servicing a profit centre. It does not seem right to me that companies try to make a profit off customers when their product breaks.
- Our salespeople are not on commission and they will never pressure you to buy a car. Their goal and the sole metric of their success is to have you enjoy the experience of visiting so much that you look forward to returning.

Silicon Valley

- I'm a Silicon Valley person. I just think people from Silicon Valley can do anything.
- I think the high-tech industry is used to developing new things very quickly. It's the Silicon Valley way of doing business: You either move very quickly and work hard to improve your product technology, or you get destroyed by some other company.
- Silicon Valley has some of the smartest engineers and technology business people in the world.

- The problem with the Silicon Valley financing model is that you lose control after the first investment round.

Simplicity

- Simplicity is a fantastic virtue but it requires hard work and diligence to achieve it and education to appreciate it. To make matters worse; complexity sells better.

Skill

- Frequently the hard skills, such as the skills that are needed for the job are much easier to teach and learn than the soft skills needed for teamwork, leadership and influence. Skills can be learned, but intention comes from within. You can't teach or train the heart.
- You can learn any skill you want for free on YouTube. You can become a person of value in a matter of months. Just a few years ago this wasn't possible. If you were fortunate enough to be born in this era, take full advantage of it.

Smart People

The most important mistake I see smart people making is assuming that they are smart.

Social Media

- I hate writing about personal stuff. I don't have a

Facebook page. I don't use my Twitter account. I am familiar with both, but I don't use them.

- I have made the mistaken assumption—and I will attempt to be better at this—of thinking that because somebody is on Twitter and is attacking me that it is open season. And that is my mistake.
- Some people use their hair to express themselves; I use Twitter.
- I think there should be regulations on social media to the degree that it negatively affects the public good.
- It is far easier to be mean on social media than it is to be unpleasant or spiteful in person.
- Facebook is quite entrenched and has a network effect. It is hard to break into a network once it is formed.
- Particularly on Instagram, people seem to have a much better life than they do. People appear to be much better-looking than they are, and they are way happier-seeming than they are.
- Generally, the view that I've had on Twitter is if you're on Twitter, you're in, like, the meme—you're in meme war land. If you're on Twitter, you're in the arena. And so, essentially, if you attack me, it is therefore fine and acceptable for me to attack back.
- There is no shortage of negative feedback on Twitter

SolarCity

- SolarCity is a giant distributed utility. It is working in partnership with the house and businesses and competition with the big monopoly utility. I think it is the power of the people.

Solar Power

- A utility can handle up to 20 per cent of production from solar and that helps the grid because it produces electricity when needed. Solar power peaks in the middle of the day and that's also when air conditioning is running and businesses are operating, so power production matches usage.
- What most people know but don't realize they know is that the world is almost entirely solar-powered already. If the sun wasn't there, we would be an ice ball at three degrees Kelvin, and the sun powers the entire system of precipitation. The whole ecosystem is solar-powered.
- The hard part of solar power is not the panel. It is the whole system. It is designing something that is going to fit on a particular rooftop, then you have got to mount the system, wire it up, connect the inverters to the grid and also you have got to do all the permitting. It is a bunch of thorny, unglamorous, and stupid problems, but if somebody doesn't optimize

them, they are still going to cost a ton of money. And many of them are not enjoyable problems. They are not exciting problems to optimize, but they are the problems that matter in the cost of solar power.

- If anyone has a vested interest in space solar power, it would have to be me.
- There are a few things that I think are really bogus. One is space mining; another is space solar power. If you calculate how much it costs to bring either the photons from space solar power back to earth or the raw material back to earth, the economics don't make sense.
- Something most people know but don't realize they know is that the world is almost entirely solar-powered already. If the sun wasn't there, we would be an ice ball at 3 degrees Kelvin. The sun powers the entire system of precipitation. The whole ecosystem is solar-powered.

Solution

- Don't delude yourself into thinking something is working when it is not or you will get fixated on a bad solution.
- Once you figure out the question, then the answer is relatively easy.
- Solar power, stationary storage and electric cars are the solutions to the Earth's needs. We are trying

to make that happen as fast as possible, and the fundamental good of SolarCity and Tesla will be measured by the degree to which we accelerate that transition.

- I think I am proficient at inventing solutions to problems. Things seem fairly obvious to me that are not obvious to most people. And I am not trying to do it or anything. It just seems I see the truth of things and others seem less able to do so.
- I care immensely about the truth of things and try to understand the truth of things. I think that is important. If you decide to come up with a solution, then the truth is really important.
- To solve the sustainable energy question, we need sustainable energy production, which is going to come primarily in the form of solar in my view. Then combine that with stationary storage and electricity, and you have a complete solution to a sustainable energy future. Those are the three parts that are needed, and those are the three things that I think Tesla should be providing.

Space

- If we drive down the cost of transportation in space, we can do tremendous things.
- I think we are at the dawn of a new era in commercial space exploration.

- For us to have a future that is exciting and inspiring, it has to be one where we are a space-bearing civilization.
- I would like to fly in space. That would be cool. I used to just do personally risky things, but now I have children and responsibilities, so I can't be my test pilot. That wouldn't be a good idea. But I want to fly as soon as it's a sensible thing to do.
- I thought nobody is going to be absurd enough to do space, so I better do space.
- Right now, on earth, you can go anywhere in 24 hours. You can fly over the Antarctic pole and parachute out 24 hours from now if you want. You can get parachuted to the top of Mount Everest from the right plane. You can go to the bottom of the ocean. On earth, from a physical standpoint, you can go anywhere. There is no real physical frontier on earth anymore, but space is that frontier.
- What I'm trying to do is, is to make a significant difference in space flight. And help make space flight accessible to almost anyone.

Space Suit

- We have spent a concerted effort on the space suit design, on both the functionality and the aesthetics. It is really hard because if you just optimize for functionality, it is one thing but if you optimize it for aesthetics, it doesn't work. Those things that you see in movies, don't work. So, it is like, "How do we make something that looks impressive and works?" with the key goal here being that when people see the space suit, we want them to think, "Yes, I want to wear that thing one day."

SpaceX

- I'm trying to construct a world that maximizes the probability that SpaceX continues its mission without me.
- To our knowledge, life exists on only one planet, earth. If something reprehensible happens, it's gone. I think we should establish life on another planet Mars in particular, but we are not making acceptable progress. SpaceX intended to make that happen.
- SpaceX has the potential of saving the US government $1 billion a year. We are opposed to creating an entrenched monopoly with no realistic means for anyone to compete.
- The original idea for SpaceX was just to have a philanthropic mission to Mars.
- On one of the SpaceX flights, we had a secret payload: a wheel of cheese. We flew to orbit and brought it back, so it was the world's first 'space cheese.' It was, in part, a tribute to Monty Python.

- I could not be prouder of everyone at SpaceX and all our suppliers who worked incredibly hard to develop, test, and fly the first commercial human spaceflight system in history to be certified by NASA. This is a great honour that inspires confidence in our endeavour to return to the Moon, travel to Mars, and ultimately help humanity become multi-planetary.
- While most rockets are designed to burn up on re-entry, SpaceX is building rockets that not only withstand re-entry but also land safely on earth to be refuelled and fly again.
- The goal of SpaceX is to revolutionize space travel. The long-term goal is to establish Mars as a self-sustaining civilization as well as to have a more exciting future.

Special Forces

- I want to accentuate the philosophy that I have with companies in the start-up phase, which is a sort of "Special Forces" approach. The minimum passing grade is excellent. That's the way I believe start-up companies need to be if they are ultimately going to be ambitious and successful companies. We adhered to that to some degree, but we strayed from that path in a few places. That doesn't mean the people that we let go on that basis would be considered bad—

it is just the difference between Special Forces and the regular army. If you are going to get through a really tough environment and ultimately grow the company to something significant, you have to have a very high level of dedication and talent throughout the organization.

Stationary Storage

- Stationary storage will be as big as the car business long term. The growth rate will probably be several times what it is for the car business.

Stock Market

- A stock market is a strange thing. It's like having a manic depressive who is constantly telling you how much your company's worth. Sometimes they have a good day, and sometimes they have a bad day but the company is the same. The public markets are crazy.

Students

- Failing students realize that school isn't everything. Failing students develop skills other than memorization. Failing students go against what the crowd says. Failing students can look past what their teachers and parents say. This is why failing students become rich.

Success

- Plan for success but be prepared to fail.
- If we hadn't responded to what people said, we probably wouldn't have been as successful.
- People either have a strategy where success is not one of the possible outcomes—occasionally it's that. And then they don't change that strategy once that becomes clear, amazingly. Or they cannot attract a critical mass of technical talent if it's in a technology-related thing. Or they run out of money before reaching a cash-flow positive situation. That tends to be what occurs.
- The ability to attract and motivate great people is critical to the success of a company because a company is a group of people that are assembled to create a product or service. That is the purpose of a company. People sometimes forget this elementary truth. If you can get gifted or inspired people to join the company and work together towards a common goal and have a relentless sense of perfection about that goal, then you will end up with a wonderful product. And if you have a great product, many people will buy it, and then the company will be successful.
- If we don't succeed, then we will certainly be pointed to as a reason why people shouldn't even try for these

things. So, I think it is important that we do whatever is necessary to keep going.

Sun

- We just need to catch an extremely tiny amount of it (the sun) to power all of civilization.

Supplier

- Generally, we find if you want something cheap, and fast, and it is probably going to work, then you should use a regular commercial supplier. If you want something expensive, takes a long time, and might work, use an aerospace supplier.

Sustainable Energy

- If we don't have sustainable energy generation, there is no way that we can conserve our way to a bright future. We have to fundamentally make sustainable energy available.

❑

Talent

- It is a mistake to hire numerous people to get a complicated job done. Numbers will never compensate for talent in getting the right answers (two people who don't know something are no better than one), it will tend to slow down the progress, and will make the task incredibly expensive.
- The biggest mistake, in general, I have made, is to put too much of a weighting on someone's talent and not enough on their personality. And I have made that mistake several times. I think it matters whether somebody has a warm heart, it does. I have made the mistake of thinking that it is sometimes just about the brain.
- I do not fire talented people; you know unless there is no option and not without warning.
- Talent is extremely important. It's like a sports team, the team that has the best individual player will often

win, but then there's multiplayer from how those players work together and the strategy they employ.

- Do what you want to do. Don't choose a field of work because your friend or your parents recommended something. Know your talents and abilities, and create something incredible.
- Each one of us can contribute something—humour, technology, political acumen. You need to discover your potential and your unique talents, and then use them to improve the quality of life for others.
- I just want to emphasize that sometimes—in fact, most of the time—I get way too much credit or attention for what I do. I am just the visible element. But the reason those companies are successful is that we have extremely talented people at all levels that are making it happen.

Tax

- I'm anti-tax, but I'm pro-carbon tax.
- The reason we should do a carbon tax is that it's the right thing to do. It's economics 101, elementary stuff.
- Whenever you have the opportunity, talk to your politicians. Ask them to enact a carbon tax. We have to fix the unpriced externality. I would talk to my friends about it and fight the propaganda from the carbon industry.

Teacher

- The best teacher I ever had was my elementary school principal. Our maths teacher quit for some reason, and he decided to sub himself for maths and accelerate the syllabus by a year. We had to work like the house was on fire for the first half of the lesson and do extra homework, but then we got to hear stories of when he was a soldier in the Second World War. If you didn't do the work, you didn't get to hear the stories. Everybody did the work.

Technology

- There are two things required when launching affordable technology. The first is economies of scale, and the other is the need to design and iterate things. Sometimes, you might be forced to change the version periodically.
- If you look at our current technology level, something strange has happened to civilizations, and I mean strange in a negative way. And it could be that there are a whole lot of dead, one-planet civilizations.
- We built this incredible technology, but it wasn't being used by the customers in the right way. It's a bit like building F22 fighter jets and then you sell them to people and they roll them down the hill at each other. If you have outstanding technology, you

want to go all the way to the end customer. Don't sell it to some bonehead legacy company that doesn't understand how to use it.

- Disruptive technology, where you have a big technology discontinuity, tends to come from new companies.
- Large-scale manufacturing, especially of new technology, is somewhere between 1,000 per cent and 10,000 per cent harder than the prototype. I would regard, at this point, prototypes as a trivial joke.
- The key to making things affordable is design and technology improvements, as well as scale.
- People often mistake technology for a static picture. It is less like a picture and more like a movie. It's the velocity of technology innovation that matters and the acceleration.
- If you think back to the beginning of cell phones, laptops or any new technology, it is always expensive.
- What many people don't appreciate is that technology does not automatically improve. It only improves if a lot of really strong engineering talent is applied to the problem. There are many examples in history where civilizations have reached a certain technology level and then have fallen well below that and then recovered only millennia later.
- Technology will at some point be indistinguishable from reality.

Tesla

- Tesla is a small company, so it has a significant effect on the world. We have to inspire others to create compelling electric cars to the degree that we can help others; create electric cars.
- I think in the long term you can see Tesla establishing factories in Europe, other parts of the US and Asia.
- Tesla is both a hardware and software company. So, an enormous percentage of our engineers are soft engineers, and you can think of our car as a laptop on wheels.
- The safest car you can drive is a Tesla.
- The aspect I focus on at Tesla is putting all the money and attention into trying to make the product as compelling as possible because I think that the way to sell any product is through word of mouth. The key is to have a product that people will love.
- I wish we could be private with Tesla. It makes us less efficient to be a public company.
- I think Tesla will most likely develop its autopilot system for the car, as I think it should be camera-based, not lidar-based. However, it is also possible that we should do something jointly with Google.
- Tesla is here to stay and keep fighting for the electric car revolution.

- If you don't have sustainable energy, you have unsustainable energy. The fundamental value of a company like Tesla is the degree to which it accelerates the advent of sustainable energy faster than it would otherwise occur.
- We polled Tesla owners on 'do they want autopilot disabled or not.' Not one person wanted it disabled. That's pretty telling.
- I care very deeply about the people at Tesla. I feel as if I have a great debt to the people of Tesla who are making the company successful.
- Tesla is becoming a real car company.
- Tesla believes strongly in making things. We believe that manufacturing technology is itself subject to a tremendous amount of innovation, and we believe that there is more potential for innovation in manufacturing than there is in the potential of a car by a long shot. This is just a philosophical difference. Perhaps we are wrong. But we believe in the manufacturing, and we believe that a company that values manufacturing as highly as we do is going to attract the best minds in manufacturing.
- I think a Tesla is the most enjoyable thing you could probably buy ever. That's what it meant to be. It's not exactly a car. It's a thing to maximize enjoyment.
- The goal of Tesla is to accelerate sustainable energy, so we are going to take a step back and think about

what's most likely to achieve that goal. Also, if we created a patent portfolio that discouraged other companies from making electric cars then that would be inconsistent with our mission. So, we open-sourced all the patents to help anyone else who wants to make an electric car.

- I have never felt anything like Tesla's acceleration speed; it is faster than falling. It is like having your roller coaster on tap.
- Tesla's motivation is to make electric transport as affordable as possible. That is what informs all our actions. So, if we do something, and we charge for this or that, it is not because we want to make things more expensive, it is because we can't figure out how to make it less expensive.
- At Tesla, we try very hard to do the right thing. If the right thing does not happen it is because we may have made a mistake or we weren't aware of it, but we always try to do the right thing to the best of our ability.
- When people see who is investing in the IPO, it is the smartest, most long-term thinking investors in the market. It is an amazing set of investors. So, I think it is worth noting that the smartest investors in the world are betting on Tesla. They must have a reason for doing so.

Time Management

- I have not read any books on time management.
- 5 am is the hour when legends are either waking up or going to bed.

Tony Stark

- There are some important differences between me and Tony Stark; I have five children, so I spend more time going to Disneyland than parties.

Transportation

- If SpaceX and other companies can lower the cost of transport to orbit and perhaps beyond, then there is tremendous potential for entrepreneurship at the destination. You can think of it like Union Pacific Railroad. Before there was the Union Pacific Railroad, it was really hard to have commerce between the west coast and the east coast. It would go by wagon or a long sailing journey, but once there was transport, then there were huge opportunities.

Trend

- Don't just follow the trend. You may have heard me say that it's advisable to think regarding the physics approach of first principles. Which is, rather than reasoning by analogy, you boil things down to the most fundamental truths you can imagine and reason from there.

- Don't be a trend follower, be a trendsetter.

Tunnels

- The fundamental problem with cities is that we build cities in 3D. you have got these tall buildings with so many people on each floor, but then you have got 2D roads. That doesn't work. You are guaranteed to have gridlock. But you can go 3D if you have tunnels. And you can have many tunnels crisscrossing each other with perhaps of a few metres of the vertical distance between them and completely get rid of traffic problems.

❑

Universe

- The universe, as we know it, will dissipate into a fine mist of cold nothingness eventually.

❑

Vacation

- That's my lesson for taking a vacation; vacation will kill you.
- I'd like to dial it back 5 per cent or 10 per cent and try to have a vacation that's not just an e-mail with a view.

Value

- If something has to be designed and invented, and you have to figure out how to ensure that the value of the thing you create is greater than the cost of the inputs, then that is probably my core skill.

Venture Capital

- Great things will never happen with VCs (Venture Capitalists) or professional managers. They have a high drive but they don't have the creativity or the insight. Some do but most don't.

- If you have a choice of a lower valuation with someone you like or a higher valuation with someone you have a question mark about, take the lower valuation. It is better to have a higher-quality venture capitalist whom you think would be great to work with than to get a higher valuation with someone where there's even a question mark.
- I think the best way to attract venture capital is to try and come up with a demonstration of whatever product or service it is and ideally take that as far as you can. Just see if you can sell that to real customers and start generating some momentum. The further along you can get with that, the more likely you are to get the funding.

Video Games

- To make an embarrassing admission, I like video games. That's what got me into software engineering when I was a child. I wanted to make money so I could buy a better computer to play better video games—nothing like saving the world.

❑

Will

- Your will is the most accurate way to predict the future.

Work

- Work like hell. You have to work 80 to 100 hours a week. This improves the odds of success. If other people are putting in 40-hour workweeks and you are putting in 100-hour workweeks, then even if you are doing the same thing, you know that you will achieve in four months what it takes them a year to achieve.
- There are many easier places to work, but nobody ever changed the world on 40 hours a week.
- If you are a co-founder or CEO, you have to do all kinds of tasks you might not want to do. If you don't do your chores, the company won't succeed. No task is menial.

- I think it is incredibly important that you have an environment in general where people look forward to coming to work because it is just so much easier to work hard if you love what you are doing.
- We haven't got into orbit, true, but we have made considerable progress. If it is an 'all or nothing' proposition then we have failed. But it is not an 'all or nothing' proposition. We must get to orbit eventually, and we will. It might take us one, two or three more tries, but we will make it work.
- Well, we got to space. You don't necessarily go all the way on the first few dates. You have got to work your way up there.

Worrying

- If you have got weight to lose, money to make or wisdom to obtain; you should not be worried about media, celebrities or how other people live. Fix your life, then look outwards.

Wrong

- I take the position that I'm always to some degree wrong, and I aspire to be less wrong.

❑

Awards and Achievements

- In 2006, Musk served as a member of the United States National Academy of Sciences Aeronautics and Space Engineering Board.
- National Wildlife Federation 2008 National Conservation Achievement award for Tesla and Solar City.
- Listed as one of Time's 100 people who most affected the world in 2010.
- Named as one of the 75 most influential people of the twenty-first century by *Esquire* magazine.
- Recognized as a Living Legend of Aviation in 2010 by the Kitty Hawk Foundation for creating the successor to the Space Shuttle (Falcon 9 rocket and Dragon spacecraft).
- In 2010, the premier world organization for aerospace records, the 'Federation Aéronautique International' awarded Musk the 'FAI Gold Space Medal. He shares this highest honour with prominent personalities like Neil Armstrong and John Glenn.

- In June 2011, Musk was awarded the US$250,000 Heinlein Prize for Advances in Space Commercialization.
- In 2012, Musk was awarded the Royal Aeronautical Society's highest award: a Gold Medal.
- Musk was the 2012 recipient of *Smithsonian* magazine's American Ingenuity Award in the Technology category.
- He has won multiple awards and recognition for his many advancements in science, technology and business alike and in 2013 was named *Fortune* magazine's 'Businessperson of the Year for his companies SpaceX, Tesla Motors and Solar City. In June 2016, Business Insider named Musk one of the "Top 10 Business Visionaries Creating Value for the World" along with Mark Zuckerberg and Sal Khan.
- In 2016, he was ranked 21st on the *Forbes* list of The World's Most Powerful People.
- He was ranked as the 54th wealthiest person in the world in the 2018 Forbes list.
- Musk was elected a Fellow of the Royal Society (FRS) in 2018.

❑